SACRED REMNANTS

Charles Freyberg

Interactive Press
Brisbane

Interactive Press
an imprint of IP (Interactive Publications Pty Ltd)
Treetop Studio • 9 Kuhler Court
Carindale, Queensland, Australia 4152
sales@ipoz.biz
https://ipoz.biz/shop
First published by IP in 2026

Printed in 14 pt Avenir Book on Caslon Pro 12 pt.

ISBN: 9781923435308 (PB) 9781923435315 (eBook)

A catalogue record for this book is available from the National Library of Australia

Also by Charles Freyberg

Dining at the Edge (Ginninderra Press, 2018)
The Crumbling Mansion (Ginninderra Press, 2021)

INTRODUCTION

Charles Freyberg's head has many mansions, with many lodgers. These acutely caught poems, stories, and sketches are peopled by a cavalcade of queers, queens, bohemians, bums, beats, and burlesque artists from Freyberg's home patch, Sydney's Kings Cross. There are many dear fringe-dwelling friends, mostly now gone. There is the larger-than-life character of the author's beloved, and largely disappeared, King's Cross, with its ghosts of legendary venues like Les Girls and the Bourbon and Beefsteak. There is lament at how the seedy but vibrant old Bo-Ho epicenter of the Red-Light District is being 'cleaned up' into a Green Light Precinct of shiny new apartment blocks – a homogenous blandscape of gentrification squeezing out the area's character and characters.

The story circle spreads out from the 'Cross to evoke and reimagine some of the troubling colonial heritage of the author's forebears in his native Queensland, including their potential crimes against the indigenous. The book straddles time frames, homes, venues, states, and hemispheres. There are the author's reimaginings of Shakespeare from his time as a young man in London. Throughout, there is a strong bond of friendship, love, and affection for people. There is also a heady whiff of melancholy for largely disappeared places and people. So many old friends swallowed in the bohemian ether. And yet they vividly live on here, in the creative head. There are 'more stories as we drink the open wounds of this city.' Yes, there are ghosts. But this evocative and large-hearted book also speaks strongly to William Faulkner's adage that 'the past is never dead, it's not even past'.

– **Tug Dumbly,** poet

Charles refuses the obfuscation of separation and containment. There's a clue to understanding the depth and breadth of perspective in these poems from an artist/poet who unites a local within a universal towards the interaction of land, people, and language.

– **Angela Stretch,** Poetry Sydney

Praise for *The Crumbling Mansion*

The work of Charles Freyberg offers a unique perspective that can deeply connect with Spanish audiences as it explores universal themes of love, identity, memory, and human frailty.... he delves into the deep connection between nature and human sensitivity... His work resonates with Latin American literary movements that seek to include diverse sexual and gender identities, offering fresh voices and perspectives.

– **Maria del Castillo Sucerquia,** Colombian poet and translator

Much of *The Crumbling Mansion* feels like a night book, slightly surreal and immersed in a world of lights and excitement, pitched at the edge of danger, sex, and theatre. Costume and makeup glitter under lights, where creativity finds its truest form in performance.

– **Magdalena Ball,** *The Compulsive Reader*

The denizens of a crumbling mansion coil at the heart of this collection, a shifting, multivocal performance capturing an inner-city milieu frayed by time but gentle in memory. Freyberg is a fearless scribe of personal transformation and regeneration. He reignites the forgotten voices of Kings Cross and fills them with compassion and yearning. Freyberg's writing has an elasticity of purpose and subject, with loss, the knife edge of gentrification, and nostalgia clinging to plangent evocations of nature, injustice, and desire.

– **Rico Craig,** poet

Praise for *Dining at the Edge*

In Charles Freyberg's dislocated world, we "gather cracks" in life's journey that demand both attention and love. In *Dining at the Edge*, we are confronted by scenarios of loss and degradation, but also a profound joy in art as solace. In the poems, there is ambiguity and subtlety, as well as intensely realised, high-key images that surprise and confront. Freyberg writes through a compelling voice that aches and celebrates—and in this, he proclaims the imperatives of love.

– **Simeon Kronenberg,** poet

Charles Freyberg entices us into a midnight world where passion brings both rapture and peril. Like Kenneth Slessor, Dorothy Hewitt, and Michael Dransfield, he portrays the creative denizens of Kings Cross after dark with lyrical poems mourning the devastation wrought by addiction, plague, and madness.

– **Lou Steer,** poet and member of Fierce Violet

Cover design: John O'Driscoll

Book design: David P Reiter

Author photo: John O'Driscoll

Photo of the author's great-great-grandfather Joseph Macarthy: Oxley Collection, State Library of Queensland

Contents

This book is dedicated to my beloved friend
Stephen Edwards (1954–2025)

PART ONE

Mavericks and Divas

written on Gadigal Country,
energised by sixty thousand years of continuous storytelling

PART ONE

Mavericks and Divas

TO ELIZABETH BURTON

Kings Cross Sydney on Gadigal Country

I'm sixteen
but not very sweet
my body knotted
in this raucous place
of jarring rhythms
where women gyrate
into a blur of hair and flesh.
My gawky friends have dragged me here
so far from my cocoon
I want quiet
my books shining with striking phrases
lines of trees in my window
but here
my head revolves
I echo their whistles and grunts
they dig me in the ribs
they are amazed
I'm empty
I'm not a man
I shout even louder
I stare at them
I want to be their mirror
I feel so alone
are they all pretending, too?
and then

a swirl of colour
strands of brightening fabric leap
a sweep of long hair
my clenched arms loosen
as her arms open in a welcoming
she sheds her layers
down to the warmth of her body
then she slows
gracefully standing and sharing
her blue eyes playful.
She's smiling just at me
She knows how I need that smile
so awkward and alone.

My lips loosen from their pout
as something gathers within me
hidden and gorgeous
bursting through my check shirt.
She really sees me
I'm squirming in my chair
my arms gyrate
as my friends look at me and laugh.
She gathers her clothes and leaves
with a gentle wave.

As we walk out
to the chaos of the street,
I feel the sweetness of my body
in the wind.
I felt a yearning to share myself
with intimacy, with beauty

like Elizabeth.
I cannot tell my friends.
If only I could kiss them.

Painting by Kate Vidgen, oil on canvas, in the poet's collection

TO KATE

A shrill warmth through the intercom—
I'd heard you were dead.
Then I hesitate, not sure I want you to reappear
in a chaos you drag around everywhere.

You float through the door,
waves of ginger hair with grey flecks at the roots
a purple headband can't restrain it.
Green eyes flash around the room
heightened in running mascara.

You see me. Now you're anchored.

Wide open eyes
stare deeply inward.
Your head is like a painted porcelain egg
it's balanced on multi-coloured streams of fabric,
your body is hidden in a rare bird's plumage.
Your lips are pursed, unable to speak
your arm is reaching for something you cannot find
your legs are a wheel; your journey is precarious.

I'm staring at your painting hanging on my wall.
Then I see you.

Full orange lips burst open in a smile
showing brown and broken teeth.

We hug, a sour smell on your clothes.
Laddered green stockings, frayed lace of petticoat,
layers of op shop treasures. You shiver, it's winter
but there's a bead of sweat on your brow.

Your lips pursed, a fury in your eyes.
We laugh, but it's hollow. We fall silent.
You are so vulnerable as I am too
as we feel them gathering. A flash
of bleached hair, the dark riff
of a bass guitar, mischievous eyes—

fragments of people we've loved.
We channel their words; can they still enliven us?

My voice rises; my gestures widen just like yours.
The blandness of my t-shirt is not enough
to contain my stories; I want a colourful cape
a band in my hair, orange on my lips,

a reflection of you as you conjure a man
you loved in a forest paradise.

He's shaking with fury, his body fills the room
your fists clench – my body
tightens – a clown is spitting
poison, his breath stinks
as he slices me open, I'm nothing.
We stare as they batter us
we collapse together – laughing –

Then silence.

I look at your painting, your shadow,
I love it. You wrap me in your arms
you pour another drink.

We're surrounded by flowers in a purple forest
like a medieval tapestry. Eyes are staring from the heart
of the flowers, we are being scrutinised, beauty
is full of malice. Colourful layers of fabric
cling to our bodies like memories,

a mingling of genders within—
to make a gorgeous vessel
to contain our stories,
a wheel takes us to wherever.

We're fragile like painted eggs.
One day you fell. Now I shape
the curves and lines of these words,
a motley for my next performance.

JESSIE IN FISH PARK GARRAGUL (ELIZABETH BAY)

We're silent
as a carp
orange like a juicy fruit
lifts their tail and splashes
the clear pool,
their body wobbles
then shoots through the water,
a second fish shines in silver
like a reflection
playing in unison beside them
their lover.
They're not male or female but both,
scales gleaming as they move
like your inflating breath
in your slim expressive body.

Your hair is long, as orange as the fish,
a scab from a fight on their glowing flesh,
the silver is tarnished with purple
like our inner scars and blemishes.
I take your hand and your body
twirls around me in dance.
Your eyes are marbles
irises speckled green and brown,
bright in the dusky light.
We do not need to speak.

A cloud is floating above the harbour.
What's it like? A rabbit?
We see pointy ears, pom pom tail
casting a shadow on the steel of the water.
The sun sits behind them like a lamp
their coat is brightening.
You smack your lips like a cartoon bunny
shadows of whiskers on your face,
your fur a brightly coloured T-shirt.
You lie down on the ground
I lie down beside you.
We're breathing the carp, the lilies in the pool,
the tiny white flowers spangled round the water's edge.
Your head rests on my chest
my mind stops whirring with anxiety.
The idle boasting of surrounding apartments ceases.

TO MAE

It was a chilly dusk
in springtime when I sensed her presence
just past Fish Park, a place she loved.
Buds were changing into purple blossoms,
opening up my imagination.
As I pass her flat in a grand old building
a bony hand is shaking in mine;
the tap of a stick,
a tongue protrudes
from a pagan mask with staring eyes
a bird in flight is spinning on a mobile.
I see her fascinations in figments,
the window is empty, everything is gone.
I realise she's asking me to remember her.

I'm sitting in her spacious living room.
A wicker basket full of stones;
tiger's eye and amethyst shine.
I pick one up, her painted lips move
and she takes me to a cave in Spain.
Cats and birds in coloured glass,
a giant wooden bison, then a giraffe
black blotches on orange. I touch it, it wobbles.
Clouds drifting over mountains in a painting;
her long lunches with the artist.
"He was such a hilarious lush!"
I see a shock of white hair

cascading over her shoulders;
she's sipping cognac
surrounded by a dazzle of fragments
until we pause at a photograph
sitting alone on a lacquered table beside her,

a young man in black and white from long ago.
His eyes are full of mischief,
her deep blue eyes awaken, sparkling.
His lips are frozen in a flirtatious smile.

"He's beautiful," I say, "So like you."
"He was my brother."

I'm walking her up the hill
holding her bony hand.
Her back is hunched,
she shuffles painfully
her voice shakes.
There's an energy still coiled within,
she's still impulsive, but her body resists.

"It's so ghastly to be old!"
To me, she embodies a remarkable life.
Her face is like parchment;
the flourishes of her adventures
are etched deeply into it,
framed by her chaotic white hair.
As we're sitting by the photo,
I gesture eloquently as I tell
of some man who frustrates me.

My hair is long and unkempt like hers.
She laughs. Do I remind her of her brother?

I'm now in my studio,
crammed with art and quaint memorabilia
every object a story
from my travels, the people who've inspired me.
I'm alone, an eccentric,
surrounded by precious remnants.
I hear her voice
the lines on her face quiver as she laughs.
The photo winks. I can hear them together.

I pick up my pen.

"He woke me up.
My bedroom was plush.
I was surrounded by textbooks
dainty teddy bears and dolls,
no longer a little girl, but not yet a woman.
His clothes were caked with mud,
bruises on his neck, the buttons torn from his shirt.
It was so late. He was 16, full of precocious spontaneity.

'Those American soldiers are so wild!' he said.
'They love me!' Then he burst into tears.
'Don't tell Mummy and Daddy!'
'About what?'
There was no word.
Whatever he'd done was beyond my vocabulary
but I understood.
He was exhilarated.

The solid tables, the velvet drapes
the tired chatter of our parents, our daily rituals
were just a cocoon he'd ripped open
with his vitality. I knew he'd be hurt.
I smoothed some foundation over his blemishes."
(She never did tell them.)

"He's at the piano.
His playing shimmered with yearning.
I'd sing along,
I wanted to be a diva.
Only in music could we be honest
about our rebellion,
seeking the rapture and danger of love.
He was flirtatious and gentle
in a purple blazer
playing requests in bars,
conjuring somewhere

way above the chimney tops
where his loving could shine,
desires that couldn't be stated.
He'd wink at all the lonely men.
They understood. I understood.
We'd go to musicals, coyly mouthing the words
and then to the opera, enraptured by forbidden love."
(Sixty years later, you took *me* to the opera.
We gasped at our favourite arias, like you and your brother.)

"I enrolled in university,
one of the only women in 1948.

The men were constricted
stuffed shirts held up by braces.
I'd talk to them about Balzac and Zola
about the energy and rebellion in Paris
about Sydney, so full of prejudice and restriction.
They'd yawn. They only watched each other.

They never listened to their own impulses,
learning how to conform, with a woman in the kitchen.
They'd shut me up with an ugly pass at the end of the night;
I didn't want them.

He'd call me some nights,
and I'd go to the police station.
Cuts and bruises on his face,
frightened by vile abuse.
These men wanted to neuter him.
I'd post his bail, bathe his wounds
sit next to him in court.

He was so much braver than any of them
so much more a man,
the rich lilt in his voice so free and cheerful
playful and precocious, how he made me laugh!
I'd lend him the clothes
and we'd go to secret parties where all rules were reversed.
He was much more of a woman, too.

"The men who wanted to crush him
wanted to crush me. I wouldn't let them!

I'd follow my fascinations, just like him.
I studied archaeology, ancient art
the beginnings of human self-expression.
He'd go to parks at night, knotting with shadows
in a dance of pleasure, the rites of Bacchus.
He never stopped exploring.
I never stopped studying.

Oh, I married.
At first, my husband tolerated my interests
but then he was never there,
always throwing away money at the racetrack
and on whores. I left him, took the children.
"Where's his picture?" I ask.
She points to the bin and snorts.
"I went to the opera with my brother instead.

Liberation was coming, but he was getting older.
He found love, lost it, found it again.
Full of exhilaration, then in tears.
He couldn't hold onto a job.
He was a drunk, he'd been hurt too much.
I'd show him a sculpture I was studying; he'd hug me.
He was still my inspiration; he was delighted for me.

"Then I was in Spain
exploring the caves painted with the first human art.
I could crawl through them
I was small
collecting bones and stones,
seeing the explosive colour of stencilled hands

bison and giraffes
etched in the rock.
I was the leader in my field

the only woman.
I held my nose when General Franco came to dinner.
I reared my children in an atmosphere of learning.
Look at these astonishing face masks.
I kept a stone from everywhere I went."

I visited her in the nursing home.
All the stones, the cut glass, the brilliant paintings
were gone. The only thing she had left was

her brother's photo, sitting on the enamelled table.
We'd go to lunch, her bony hand in mine
to talk about music, Spain, and her brother.
Her blue eyes sparkled.
They'd tamed her hair; it was brushed,
tied with ribbons and ponytails.
Those coils of energy, trapped in a shrunken hunched body,
were gentler now. She knew she didn't have much longer.

RATTLER

This city stifles me.
I want to be heard.
I need a place
to diverge from the normal,
where vulnerability is strength.
I'm in a pocket of crumbling warehouses;
the walls are daubed with tags.
Staring faces confront me, swirling with colour.
I glimpse sprawling sculptures
welded from discarded iron through half-open doors.
Plans have been drawn up
the wrecking ball looms

to build more cubicles of concrete and glass.
But here, for now, is the entrance to the Rattler.
The ceiling soars; a rainbow of light
reflects from the crystals of a chandelier.
Vintage couches with buttoned leather,
pierced noses, lively eyes, hair in dreadlocks
a chatter of anticipation, bodies alert in bright clothing.

I have a poem,
a piece of enlivening eccentricity
I was compelled to write.
I want to channel a dead friend
to bring them to life in my body.

Candy is the host
I feel her presence.
A silence as she stands, about to begin.

She blesses the First Nations people.
Her head shaved
she's fighting cancer.
She speaks with the urgency of a lover.
Her truths shock
but she's gentle,

her eyes are a caress as she welcomes us all.
"Let's banish the language of brutality!
This is a sacred space,
A place of love, pure love."

Trumpets and clarinets keep rhythm with drums
as she raps her song,
whispering poetry onto flesh
with delicate kisses, bodies gasping, writhing in sweat.
We picture our loving at its most intense.
I adore you, Candy, as I remember your words.

Next, a solemn woman in a gleaming red dress
is standing at the mic. She tells of a man
maddened with booze swinging his fists.
Tears in her eyes, fury in her voice
but as she recites, she glows.
She's standing here; she's survived,
her bruises fall away as we cheer.

Their flowing hair is in ponytails.
They tell of a boy tormented in a country town.
They get on the train with nothing
except their dreams of transformation,
and here they are, speaking to us, gorgeous.
They pity their attackers, the small minds.

She was stolen from her mother,
dragged screaming away by cops,
brought up by strangers,
but after years of searching,
she finds her, a moment of hesitation, then her embrace.
Still wounded, she breathes in her arms.

A guitarist in a cape and face paint
takes us on a journey with all the wild complexity
of creating in the moment.
The rage of his demons turns into yearning
as he wraps them in his music.
He overcomes. He stands there with joy.

Outside
they're disaffected and ignored,
but in here there's hope; a faith in change.
It's my turn.
I'm fat and middle-aged,
but I have a story, the audience senses it.

I'm shaking as I face them.
I feel a pool of empathy;
my poem blossoms,
my dead friend leaps to life as

we reshape the world with glamourous lies.
Non-binary before the word,
she's their sister too.

More stories as we drink
the open wounds of this city
shift into love.
Ah, those nights at the Rattler,
they don't happen anymore.
Candy Royalle is gone.
I need to find a place where…

TO THE BOURBON AND LES GIRLS.

1.
Ayesha

On a cloudy Saturday,
they walk with purpose
between gourmet food stands
in designer sandals, Italian shoes.
The people of my community meet and greet–
they're hidden behind zany sunglasses,
you can't look them in the eye.
They keep the appropriate distance
a cheery hi, a quick wave without slowing.
It's the Fitzroy Gardens markets.

Until
a flash of white
the sun emerges
she opens her arms in greeting
not for me – for everyone, for being alive,
wrapped in a translucent cape.
Her little dog licks her hand
then it snaps, baring its teeth.
Her face is a living mask

with furrows and lines engraved
by years of playfulness.
Her eyes sparkle, heightened with mascara.
She's riding in a motorised wheelchair

like it's a limousine. I leap
screaming her name. She gives me a wink,
glowing like she's about to start her show.
The milling throng freezes for a moment;
she's happy to be noticed
next to the Fountain, the Bourbon and Les Girls behind her.

2.

I pass them back and forth
twice a day, the Bourbon and the Empire
my head down, I don't want to see
how forlorn they are
waiting for the wrecking ball.

Some days I'll glimpse a sparkle
of multi-coloured sequins, a slash
of purple lipstick twisted into a smile
against the ugly grey cladding, hovering.
As I stand and focus

the surface peels away, it used to be white;
THE EMPIRE fades
now LES GIRLS is shouting again in black.
The walls are transparent, quivering.
A smoky room is packed.
She's always there, waiting to begin.

She stands like a lover
itching for a fight
painted lips widen to an O
then a flirtatious smile.

She dares us all to join her
as music soars and plummets
in waves of yearning.
Long lashes flutter, her eyes gleam with irony—
THIS IS ME, I'M OVER THE RAINBOW.

3.
Queensgate Website

Is this really all you want?
A vision, a rich collaboration
in overstuffed cushions, the spunky curve
of couches in gleaming marble,
velvet benchtops, gilded shower heads
as images jump and blur
brief as my attention span.
A place of aspiration, an enviable lifestyle
a mission statement to maximise comfort.

4.
Les Girls

She opens her arms.
a collective gasp
sprinkled with titters and groans.
She's sharing her excess—
her costume layered with leopard, glitter, and lace,

ostrich feathers bouncing on her head,
stamping feet, the faint-hearted leave.
I'm your fantasy
hidden deep beneath your buttoned shirts
your dresses off the rack, leaping from your handbags.

You bullied me in the playground
now I've transformed.
This is what it's like to be alive.
She wrestles with us
as hands start clapping, hoots and cheers
as a heckler panics and shouts

she slashes him with her razor tongue,
her voice deep, oozing with sarcasm.
He's silenced in a wave of laughter.

The dancers multiply—
muscular bodies in shining satin,
the clatter of stilettos
shadows of pink and orange on their cheeks.

5.
Bourbon and Beefsteak

Today it's sensible chat
to tiresome songs from a cover band.
They sit at gleaming tables
sharing another ordinary day.
It's just THE BOURBON now,
but wait
a flicker of chaos
the word BEEFSTEAK is alight
in bleeding neon,

a shadow behind the surface.

I close my eyes, sitting by the fountain.
I hear howls
jostling to break through the cacophony,
love songs rolling with shouts
blaring horns
the traffic revs, faces leer from car windows.
On the pavement bodies
bounce together and sparkle,

sweeping gestures in a chain reaction
from safari suits, check shirts, brightening frocks.
A lost boy longs to merge with them all
even as he despises the multi-coloured herd,
another staggers and drops in the gutter.
Swivelling heads are searching for a mate.
They're here to unwind from

endless repetition at their desks,
the yawning tidiness of their living rooms.
It's time to dive into the aquarium
with sharks and brightly squirming fish.
The music thumps then quietens to a soothing
then thumps again, the ceiling soars,
flashing lights in primary colours
mix against darkening purple.
Feathered Indian headdresses shake like seaweed,
vintage Zippo lighters, stock whips glued to the columns,

a stuffed grizzly bear shot by the publican
stands guard like a bouncer, snarling.
Books in soft leather are shelved in the alcoves.

6.
Queensgate Website

Is this all you really want?
A model laughing with wind in her hair,
gleaming concrete punctured with glass
life without limits.

The worldwide buzz of real estate,
every word conjures its opposite.
Apartments that energise
feed your smug complacency,
a mythology retold and amplified.
A dozen status markers in every photo.
An orchid in a vase, a never-opened book on art,
shapely chrome chairs in white leather.
People dwarfed by lofty ceilings
staring at yachts on the harbour,
their teeth are perfect, their fashion
a colourful motley from Westfield franchises.
They lounge around as they eat off bone china;
the applause is polite, the smiles are tame.
Bodies drained of spontaneity,
no hoots of delight or spiralling dances.

Divas and eccentrics are unwelcome here.
They cannot find the price of admission.
It's no longer a place to transform yourself—
you are your surroundings, an endless website.

7.
Les Girls

The show repeats
dancers come and go.
Some dance every night for years
their presence enlarging,
lost boys finding themselves as divas.
The designers unleash their mayhem.
A glamour challenges the city's dullness.
It's time to change, to imagine.

I pass the building back and forth
day after day, year after year
between the station and my flat
along with thousands of others.
Could it be the songs, high kicks, and pirouettes
are etched into the walls

like swirls in a tree trunk,
shaped by decades of heatwaves, pollution, wind, and storms?
Is the story of its past preserved,
buried deep in brick and masonite?
On days I'm open to dreaming

fragments hover on the walls.
I glimpse a glowing sequin, a slash of
purple lipstick twisting into a smile,
I remember the stories.

8.
Bourbon and Beefsteak

It's a place where the senses rearrange;
the normal flies away in strange tangents.
Men build to a crazed exuberance
schooner by schooner,
the women bare their shoulders
flowers on dresses leap as they laugh,
glowing cocktails in their hands.
They all sprawl at tables cackling,

chewing into half-kilo Texan steaks.
Lips drip with blood and
butter from jacket potatoes.
Can they reach the moment
where men merge
like celebrating heroes, unbuttoned shirts

stained with wine, the schoolboys
no longer gawky, the middle-aged feel young again
hunting, shaking fists, a howl of triumph?
A gentle kiss escalates
mouths slurp and tangle,

a man is pushed as they circle, spoiling for a fight.
All of Sydney loses its boundaries,
stockbrokers, sailors, rough bush yahoos
share winks, grunts, and stories.

The two worlds sometimes meet.

A famous cricketer gropes a performer from Les Girls;
he's thrown on the street, much laughter.
They wobble out in groups

flinging their arms at taxis
returning to the tidy yawn of the suburbs.
They awake in pain
and wonder if it was all a dream.

9.
Are there other ghosts?

Juanita Nielsen goes to meet a gangster
in his office at Les Girls and is never seen again.
Can we hear her last scream
telling us of the city's corruption?

I loved to hate the Bourbon.
It was the end of the road.
I often stopped for a nightcap
on my way back from Oxford Street,
enlivened by the women and shameless masculinity.
These images are etched in the Spanish arches;
so many stories and uncomfortable memories flow.
Soon it will be replaced by overpriced dullness,
no trigger left for the stories.

10.
Queensgate Website

At the pinnacle
the CEO,
smiling like a slug in a suit,
bloating himself on impoverished imaginations
adding to his pipeline of properties.
He builds up profits with his partners,
champagne and caviar with movers and shakers.
Real estate is the dream,
a mythology told and retold
all other stories erased.
When the buildings are demolished,
will all their stories be homeless?
Or will some stockbroker be awakened
by the pounding of stilettos,
by Juanita's bloodied corpse?

I sit in Fitzroy Gardens.
Ayesha opens her arms, glowing in white.

DARLING HARBOUR IN LOCKDOWN.

It's midnight
the water ripples
with a spume of yellow and blue
descending into blackness.
A half-moon is faint next to THE STAR
in glowing bold
and the endless procession of lamps
spaced equally on the beige promenade.

Behind me
opaque windows multiply, wrapped in concrete
curving and straightening with girdles of neon.
The buildings jostle for attention, repeating, repeating
weighing down the hill, which is tallest, which is newest?
I gasp. What hugeness they have, gathered together!

LOGOS SHOUT, slick shapes in rainbow colours.
They each gleam their billions, cold and brutal
above revolving doors to marble lobbies
wreathed with orange grapes in garlands.
The doors are still, the lobbies are frozen,
the city is unpeopled!

The wind whistles, the water laps
a hungry seagull glides, a masked man waves,
his dog bares its teeth; the city is just an ornate shell!
I am breathing deeply, full of weird imaginings.

Behind grey rows of windows, glowing banks of synapses
still breed money without us, humming with everything we do or know.
No gaggles of harried pinstripes pouring in, pouring out
only empty designer chairs, fridges shining with unreachable
drinks.

I feel oddly cheerful. I stride the beige promenade.
None of this has ever mattered to me,
is it all a destruction I have inflicted?
Ahead a shadow on top of the hill.
That is what I want to explore.

WATCHING MARDI GRAS 2023

to Stephen Edwards

Two aging gays with a dog
(come on, we're only sixty!)
in the midst of a swarm
everyone so much younger,
filling the street for the parade.
We've never been spectators—
isn't it about us?

We've always been in it—
shouting for a cause
or at a dinner in bad drag
celebrating in defiant style
or we've kept away, cherishing our fantasies,
hating the gawkers, the crowds
now surging for a view,
shepherded by cops in uniform.

Then the bikes roar
the music thumps
crisscrossing colour reaches into the sky,
but we're stuck behind rows
of arms waving from sensible dresses,
bodies jostling, stretching with anticipation.
The hairdos are tidy, but eyes glow with excitement
then with frustration; they cannot see
what the whole city has burst from their living rooms to see.

We wonder why we bothered, then I realise—
we're not here to see the parade
we're here to see the others.

Decades of parades replay in my mind.
Golden fans wave, sequins blur into sequins
drag queens are streaming with multicolored trains
held high by pretty boys in leather,
their lips twisting with cheekiness – I'm your Goddess tonight.
Bigots sliced open, a severed head,
the city upside down in grotesque parody
of the stuffed shirts who want to hurt us—

a hundred Chelsea Mannings, Oscar Wildes, Alan Turings
men arrested in toilets, beaten by police,
all marching proud; oppression explodes into glamour.

We revel in our difference, fighting for our love.
We remember sick friends, we defy the plague—
eyes full of tears, we shout and cheer
but then I'd walk away; it was all too much.
I'd want to be alone, to search for a man
in a back room seething with bodies.

This is not the parade this crowd is here to see.
They're not here to remember or be discomforted.
They jostle full of wonder,
yearning to share–
Hallelujah!
Something has changed.

An hour ago in the marshalling area,
we saw marchers from everywhere transforming—
old and young, every shape, type, race, and gender.
Muscular bodies breathing in translucent fabric
faces painted with multicolored beads
torsos blossoming with glossy petals
soft fur like a meerkat ready to leap,
strings of pearls, delicate lycra like a second skin.
They're here to channel LOVE—

a playful creative force
weaving God and Goddess
into an image exploding from the brain,
rippling through bodies
shining through costumes
expressing the depth of desire.
This is me!
This is my lovingness.
It's vigorous and colourful.
Let me enliven you!
My kisses are so deep.
For one night, we're all united.
We're here to channel LOVE.

We're old now; I'm gasping with amazement.
The girls and boys from everywhere
pat our dog, shake us by the hand.
They want to see LOVE in action,
they're sharing in the fantasy.

And yet we still feel the scars and the fury.
We mourn the friends who cannot be here;
we quietly celebrate our difference.
We give the crowd a cheeky grin.
I shed tears as cheers rise around us.

A STONE AT FIVE FINGERS STRAND

to Peter Urquhart

It sparkles,
so I pick it up
at the northern tip of Ireland.

It's quartz,
glistening with flecks of red and blue
in a stream of clear water.
It will be a blessing

as a mist of drizzle
pierces to the skin through my jumper.
The white dunes of a beach expand
hemmed by rough dark cliffs.
Waves explode on rock,
the foam sucked back into
the ocean's freezing turbulence,
the passion of song
repeating and varying
with centuries of defiance.

And yet – as I hold the stone up in my fingers—
I see clumps of deep grass
on the undulating cliff tops.
Cows with thick orange coats
stare with curiosity, chewing cud.

A fiddle leaps, raw nerves
through the plucking of a banjo;
the story of bloodshed in nearby Derry.
Buskers play a love song in protest
under an arch in the walls.
Faces of the dead in black and grey
stare from a mural.

I see a whitewashed chapel,
delicate in the green of a field ahead.
Then a shard of granite
etched with a Celtic prayer.
All these images wrap themselves
into a small piece of quartz
flecked with red and blue.

A blessing.
I hand it to you, my friend.

WHITE HORSE

Stanford in the Vale, England
to James Velocita

The ridgeway whistles with a freezing wind.
Ahead is the moat, now just a trench
around a mound overgrown by grass.
I whirl around, I can see everywhere—
the sky is grey, twisted with strands of white.
I see houses like pebbles, clumps of bare trees,
stone towers of churches, a valley
rolling in greenness to the horizon
in flickering light, the castle like a crown
on the hill, its outline sharpening.

"We scattered his ashes here," my friend Jim tells me.
"This was his favourite place."

A kite is soaring
so tranquil in the gusting wind
its belly a glowing ember,
its wings stretch, a flicker of its tail
as it plummets, feathers pulsating
then it rises in a jolt to float
on currents of air.

Speckles in the light gather into figments.
Two boys are running, a glow on their cheeks

they're lean, nimble-footed
as comfortable here as the hovering kite.
They know every contour, every pitfall—
best friends leaping up and down the hill.

Is one of them you, Jim?
Is Martin a shadow playing at your side?
I'm awkward, far behind, this is where you grew.
You're tumbling together, chattering stories,
muscles flex as you conjure warriors
a glint of chain mail on your bodies.
You turn into knights, then
into maidens sick with love for them.

Their village sits like a miniature in fields
they cross every day to go to school.
They're reenacting tales passed down the generations
like minstrels, pretty with their lyres
they add cheeky variations and laugh.
The castle reassembles as they find it in play—
a raucous banquet, glowing iron in a forge.
Is that you, Martin, now holding a sketchbook?

White lines stretch, the lengthening limbs
of a horse in motion, etched into soft chalky soil.
I stand in the eye, spinning three times to make a wish—
dizzy in the blur of hedged fields, spiralling birds,
the castle's remnant grows; I make the wish to let
everything I see feed the vigour of my imagination.

Haunches of horses swell, shining like the grass on the hill.
Muscular torsos twist as the riders rise
from galloping bodies, searching
every crevasse, between the spreading limbs of trees
for hidden dangers, gruesome dragons,
monsters with snakes dancing from their hair.
The warriors kiss as they go into battle
lovers fighting side by side.

An artist is revealing the power of a horse's body
in lines of chalk; an offering of love.
His full lips smile with satisfaction,
his body as lively and graceful as the horse's,
he bursts into a joyous laugh.
This is the first time I've really seen you, Martin
since you died. I remember you in Sydney
painting a woman in swirling colours;
her face was yours, her dress from another time.
I see you so clearly—
now I know where you come from.

Painting by Martin Richardson, crayon and watercolour on board, in the poet's collection

MARTIN'S PAINTING

Jim.
You travel the world,
while I sit here.
You never change, naughty and elfin.
You now pour as the roast crackles.
The candles flicker as we laugh.
We hear an echo – another breath
is buoying our mirth – a sudden peel of

pure joyful anarchy – is it you, Martin?
We pick up our glasses and turn.
Are your lips flat? No, they're poising
with fullness. The muscles in your forearm
flex. Your glass is toasting us! Your body shapely,
bathed in deep blue thoughtfulness, your eyes closed.
You sit apart, alive to the moment, cheeks colouring
like a debutante, shy of our gaze.
You're waiting to laugh again, relishing
the quirky contrast of Jim and me?
Suddenly we hug – we know why we're here.

Your likeness as a woman hangs on my wall—
a moment of your fantasy, so often forgotten
following me for twenty years. Now I realise
in unconscious yearning, I've placed the candles
cooked the same roast, dusted the painting,
so you and I can find the gateway to…

…the candelabra reaches for the roof
and glows. "I'm Martin. I mean Janice.
Clarissa?"
"Just call me Charles.
I saw you when I heard your laugh."
Now you're quiet. Can I touch your thoughts?

They're prancing, lovable
their tongues barbed, plumage
textured like exotic birds,
telling their ribald stories.

There *you* are, Jim – cigarette red raw,
dressed as a whore. But Martin – you sit apart
bathed in blue, cheeks colouring, shying from gazes.
I'm Mrs. Dalloway, gentle and refined
full of secret fantasies my mask can't hide.
Are you amazed

at this drunken cacophony? Men as women
women as drag queens, carving roast meat
as someone vomits under the table.
The room expands, the focus shifts
from deep-hewn eyes sparkling
to the warmth of each eccentric face
taking us on their taunting journey,
and like me, looking for the key to you.
Have you stumbled here, sensing you belong

to escape the rushing, overpriced blandness
of the city outside? I watch you,

lips poising full, finding fuel for
the wonder of your laugh. New shapes
are beckoning, vivid from the life around us.

Like me kissing you? Now is not the time;
our thoughts grow in parallel.
Your eyes close, searching out your need.
Was it that night
you promised me a painting…

Jim? Jim? Are you okay?
Our talking stops.
We look at the picture, back to each other.
You called me one day.
Martin is dead.
You'd found him, shivering and frightened,
gasping with pneumonia. They couldn't save him.

You travel the world, and I sit here.
Mrs. Dalloway. Juggling my fantasies.
We're ever more quirky. So stubbornly
single.
We raise our glasses.

BEWITCHED IN THE PARK

Your largeness and laughter
are at home here, sprawled in the grass.
Soon witches awake – clouds blush,
smudged with haze, bent in the branches –
a time for storytelling, lounging in the park.

You tell a breakup well,
the first encounter blissful
but it quickly descends
as your lover stumbles with awfulness
and our laughter joins in hooting harshness,
then a silence when I see your sadness
and you see mine.

Raising an eyebrow, I flick it away,
and paint you a gorgeous bully
I once was besotted with, and as you listen
you sweep back long disordered hair
like Mother Earth chuckling in the grass,
hippy boy with Gothic shadows
under eyes glinting with waywardness,
your cheekbones glow, no longer jaded,
my story finds its zest from you.

Ragged with brightness,
I see you lip-syncing

Kate in wuthering, blustering moors—
“Lover man, oh where can you be?”—
then mouth wide open, astonishing high note,
lyrics patchy, but we capture the feeling.
Your head is on my shoulder
like there’s a sudden downpour
you need shelter from.

PLAYING WITH SHAKESPEARE

London 1986 and 2023

I'm here to meet myself.
I pass Grenfell Tower
wrapped in a grey sheath.
It's here the neglected of this city
were left to burn.
Close by is the pool where I swam
to ground my drifting mind.

I'm now in the street;
respectable rows of orange terraces.
The door of Number 12 is locked
but there I am, thirty-five years ago
scruffy in my duffel coat and scarf
climbing the stairs, sighing out smoke.
A woman with a pickled face and
mane of curls opens the door and stares.
I greet her, but she frightens me.

My room is tiny, single bed, window to a wall,
a mess of half-read books, I never finish them
always looking for something new to make me gasp—
all face down in a mound of unwashed clothes.
I write in my diary, repeating an endless loop.
If only – What? (the laughing brown eyes of a boy back home)
I want… I throw away the pen. I cannot speak.

(Even now, I often cannot say what I want!
After all this time, surely, I have more confidence!)

Who calls me villain, breaks my pate across
tweaks me by the nose, plucks off my beard
and blows it in my face? Who does this?
Then – as now – my dog-eared copy
of Shakespeare is open in front of me.
Shoosh, I can write for myself!

Back then, I wanted shimmering piano,
the raucous chords of a bass guitar
the howl of a mad soprano
but I can't play music here,
(it's playing now as I write)
or the fat man next door will swear and kick the wall.
I'm not allowed to invite a friend,
but here I don't have any friends.
I left them all behind, I burnt my law books.
I flew to London to find... What?

I'm left with silence, there's nothing
here even to fuel an erection
so I can touch myself.
Shall I compare this prison
where I live unto the world?
Such marvellous words,
but I cannot declaim them here.
I walk out into the night.

2.

The houses repeat;
endless rows of pompous buildings are everywhere!
So I gesture to the purple sky
it reflects the incandescence of this massive city.

My body is alive
the muscles clench in my striding legs,
the yellow of each streetlight
is edged with a rainbow
revealing the shadows of twigs and branches
bare in the freezing wind
spread in a lattice above me.
They split at random angles,

twisting with endless complexity
like veins tapering to capillaries—
living, quivering, I want to touch them
like the flesh of a smiling boy at a bar.
I speak, he does not hear—

invisible barriers are everywhere,
all I can do is stare.
And I, like one lost in a thorny wood,
who rends the thorns and is rent with the thorns,
seeking a way and straying from the way,
not knowing how to find the open air.
Such marvellous words, yes!

3.

I'm standing in a park.
A red bus passes, the traffic is sparse
the trees are shrivelled; it's past midnight.
I'm alone—
like Hamlet, like Richard—
at last I can speak.

I wait.
The words are stuck in my head.
A breath pierces deep into my belly
then deeper again,
tickling my throat—
my lips are now muscular,

spitting out your words.
my brain I'll prove the female to my soul,
my soul the father and these two beget
a generation of still breeding thoughts,
and these same thoughts people this little world.

My brain is a woman?
Of course!
My gestures widen
my voice becomes playful
she flows through my body
trying to break free.
My soul is young and muscular
I stamp my feet
I feel him in the beat of the lines,
my chest opens
my solar plexus tingles.

An audience comes to life around me—
silly beggars sitting in the stocks
a punk sneers and smiles
there's a frightened boy I met at a bar
a Kaposi Sarcoma on his face,
a scrawny clown in white face laughs—
we all walk alone, none of us belong.
My voice quietens

I can speak to them with such intimacy
as male and female merge
into a breathing rhythm of images.
It's full of nuance and surprises
like the lattice of twisting branches and twigs.

Then I sense my wicked friend Gloucester—
an envious mountain on my back,
where sits deformity to mock my body.
So you can't get the cool boys, either
you're awkward and badly dressed—
they look right through you at the bar.

They will love me when I get the crown!
Was ever man in this humour woo'd?
Was ever man in this humour won?
I'll have him, but I will not keep him long!
I'm so much more alive than any of them!

As I speak a bunch of misfits
mavericks and addicts are applauding me.
These are my audience, my people.

I preen myself and swagger.
I'm powerful, I'm beautiful!

Hamlet joins hands with me.
Do I want to be him, or fuck him? Both!
It goes heavily with him
this majestical roof fretted with golden fire
appears a foul and pestilent congregation of vapours.
Oh, that's how I feel,
but with me at your side
you'll find your resolution
and kill your bloody bawdy villain of an uncle!

Gloucester and Hamlet kiss
I recite them in turn.
My lips are rouged,
I twirl in the streetlights
a cape flows from my shoulders.

Oh, Shakespeare, how I love your mavericks!
I still don't know what I want,
but now I can find my own words—
I don't need yours.

F

I fell for him.
It was full-on.
He was a fragrant fellow
effeminate but fierce
physically perfect,
flapping angelic wings.
We flew through the fields
as fleet as falcons
we fell into flowers.
His flesh was firm,
his front was furry
he was frisky,
I was fiery.
It was such fun.
My fetish
was to fellate his fingers.
Then he flagellated me,
flinging fresh figs and fruit at me.

But we fought
he flirted with everyone.
It was flagrant
I was flighty.
My head was full of phantoms.
In a frenzy
I called him a frivolous freeloader.
He called me a fanatic,

frightening like a fiend
huffing and puffing.
I was furious.
He wanted to be free of me.

He was a fop
in the finest flashy fashion.
He flounced through the forest,
finding other fervent followers.
I'm a physicist
I add up figures.
I find the final form of the firmament.
He was effervescent
he fluttered and fizzed,
floating in fictions.

I festered, he flowed.
Finally, he finished it.
"Let's just be friends," he fumed.
That was fatal.
I followed him
I confined him in my fetid flat.
His flesh is now foul
in a frame.
I fling fresh fruit at him.

PART TWO

MY FAMILY AND QUEENSLAND

EVONNE

We're all slumped in corded velvet.
My aunt is a flash of purple
in jagged, red-rimmed glasses,
long legs muscular
from skiing behind the boat.
She ruffles my hair,
still damp from the long blue pool
with her diamond fingers.
There's custard on my lips;
she scoops me more raisins and cherries.
She picks me up and laughs
as we whirl brightly around the room.
I've been throwing a frisbee with her boys;
it wobbles and glows. I leap—
too late, it flies and crashes.
Bang! Bang! You're dead.
They're the cowboys, I'm the Indian
I'm smaller than them.
They're showing me the way.
My parents have left me here for a whole weekend!

A walnut television brightens.
Margaret strides on long legs,
swinging her racquet.
One of the boys is larking,
my aunt shuts him up with a cuff to the head.
She lets out a whooping cheer

and then a chant
in rhythm with the game:
EVONNE GOOLAGONG IS HOPELESS,
MARGARET COURT IS FANTASTIC,
clapping hands, a dig to my ribs.
My lips begin to move
I start to say it
but the words dry
as I see Evonne.

She glides across the court,
her whole body stretching.
Her swing seems gentle
but the ball flies.
She waits, she leaps, she smiles
she loses a point
she serves again
she playfully deflects
Margaret's speed, her raw power.

My aunt sends me a winning smile
when Margaret takes a set.
"Join us!" yell at her, belittle her.
My uncle, aunt, cousins
weave together, shouting and gesturing
but Evonne becomes more graceful,
hecklers don't matter.
She rips open the cocoon—
the lounge room, the house, the garden outside
disintegrate
and only Evonne is there.

I'd never seen anything like her
in my sleepy liquid amber street
in the rumble of the playground
in the books I read,
always set far away.
My aunt offers me more pudding
I can find no words; I eat greedily.

In the schoolyard,
when the boys steal my lunch
and pass it between them
just out of reach,
when I want to join but can't
when something seems wrong
but I don't know why—
Can I find a grace like hers?

My aunt drives me home,
a cheerful flash of purple
in jagged, red-rimmed glasses.
Thank you, Evonne.
I needed to see you then.

GLASSHOUSE MOUNTAINS

on the border of Jinibara and Gubbi Gubbi Land.

At first
I see shadows
in the falling storm clouds
beyond the sodden purple flowers
blooming near the lookout rail,
but then
as the rain turns to drizzle,
the shroud brightens.
Dark rounded shapes
and a headless neck
loom in now transparent whiteness.

A panorama opens up below
as the clouds are illuminated
with slashes of white sunlight.
Homesteads on tamed pasture
are overshadowed by giant rocks:
glistening trachyte, rhyolite, granite
speckled with crystals
stubbled with shrubs.
They erupted as lava from the plain
and now are frozen in time,
a reminder of the Earth's turmoil.

The rain has stopped.
A pair of breasts on a grassy torso
sit side by side
next to a towering limb,
then a massive dome
wrapped in jostling droplets drifting
over trees and rugged faces.
Awesome presences in a translucent cloak.

Always was, always will be…

MY GREAT-GREAT-GRANDFATHER

1.

Maleny, Queensland, on Gubbi Gubbi Country

Is this how you want to be remembered?
Your stare tells of decades
of obsession in ghostly black and white.
I find you disconcerting; I share your DNA.
The fabric of your suit is furrowed with creases
caked with mud, your thick white beard
never shaven or styled, your lips fixed, refusing to smile.

An invader standing rigid like a soldier,
you came to a rainforest high on a hill
overlooking the Glasshouse Mountains. You had a vision.
Year after year you hacked and hacked, chopped and felled.
Your hand is on a dray hewn from raw timber

'First wheels on the range', wrapped in iron,
worn from dragging trunk after trunk
through brambles and mud, a wasteland
of stumps, branches, and withering vines
as your grasses sprout and burgeon, cattle fatten
and multiply, dead timber is shaped
into a homestead, milking sheds, nail by nail, beam by beam.
Your wife bears fourteen children; they're vigorous, tearing down
more of the range. No hiding place for the Gubbi Gubbi,
they scatter as you raise the iron of your gun.

You stare with a glint of exhilaration
at what you've done: you came in poverty
from the trauma of Ireland, you're a rich man.
You stand in grasses, a forest remnant behind you.
You can buy a hundred-pound bull from Jersey.
You do not care for a manicured beard or a fine tweed coat.
You're a man always moving, a fanatic;
there's still so much to be done.

2.

Kings Cross, NSW on Gadigal Country

I sit in my study
as I conjure you from a ghostly photograph,
fallen leaves of notes, books with coloured markers.
Now you're on my laptop looking back at me
my great-great-grandfather
destroyer of forest and killer!
Your stare does not apologise.

Do I despise you?
Do you find me disconcerting too?
Can I swap a favourite photograph for yours?
I'm performing in white face paint,
purple lipstick, a flowing black cape
stitched with multi-coloured strands,
speaking in jagged images as I channel
people I've loved. I find my power
in hilarious women, men searching
for inspiring men, moments of wild intimacy.

Do you want to murder me?
Aren't you a little bit proud of me?
As I write, I'm unshaven, as scruffy as you.
My work grows, day after day, year after year.
I have your determination; the task is what matters.
There's something of your voice in me, your rhythm,
one day I'll perform you if I find the right makeup.

Perhaps I wear blinkers like you.
I live in a callous city, finding my vision in a cocoon.
The Gubbi Gubbi people were forgotten
after you stole their land. I keep walking
with my head down past the homeless in the street
as lavish new apartments rise up all around me.

You tell me: your lifetime of work
produced wealth, allowing me the leisure
to judge you from a desk at the centre of a teeming city.
As we chat together, double great-grandfather,
I feel an uneasy contempt for you, and you feel it for me.

CEDAR CUTTING

The land resists.
Our machetes hack
a tangle of nameless brambles,
swathes of ferns.
We're covered in pungent earth and leaves
then a giant with grey bark flaking
revealing an orange hue,
a fat enough trunk for a Governor's banquet
on swirling lines of burnt honey.
The trunk's rough surface towers through
ropes of twisting vines
entangled in boughs splitting away
far above the squelch of mud.
We swing our axes, tearing open
a deep wedge, insert a plank
oozing with orange sap,
and we climb
through dangling creepers
and finding a shaky balance,
we rip the teeth of a two-handed saw
through the bough,
no wobble, no stumble –
the saw screeches through
the last stubborn notch of wood.
For a moment, the huge bough
is suspended; it trembles,
pulling at the strands of vines

entwined around the surrounding branches.
They stretch and rip away
with a keening squeal,
then a boom as a chunk of canopy
crashes, now open to sunlight.
The trunk is now ready to fell.
Birds are shrieking.
Cockatoos fly high and scatter
a wombat runs.
We wrap the trunk in chains
and bring up a team
of panting buffalo to drag it away
down the path cut by our machetes.
Now at last there is space.
The money from the trunk
will buy us cattle.

MANSIONS AT WEYBA LAKE

As soon as the blacks
were close enough,
the men opened fire.

Wrap-around balconies,
wicker chairs, gourmet barbecues
look out over a deep pool
tiled with blue porcelain,
a statue of Venus, pissing garden gnome.

The rain pours
running down my cheeks.
I want a place to sit and mourn.

they set up one man as a decoy
to draw the natives from the mangroves
the lake ran red with blood.

I want to sit beside the lake,
its pungent mud, twisting mangroves.
Crabs scuttle
the brackish water ripples with fish.
The killers knew where they gathered:
a holy place
where the creek meets the lake,
scattered with middens and bones from feasting,
now erased by—

Up and down the street
the mansions swell,
sweeping driveways in beige
Audis and climb-on mowers spill out
from triple garages,
tame lawns with tasteful sprays
of flowers and greenery,
floor-to-ceiling windows
pulsing with rainbow light,

then a whispering of words
read in the hush of a public library
forming into phantoms–

they chased them down and
shot them as they tried to escape
they waded into the lake

It happened near here,
but I cannot reach the lake,
it's now all private property.
I cannot walk through it,
all my upbringing—
I cannot walk through.
I'm paralyzed.
The rain is drenching.
I want to throw up.
All that's left is a dreaming assembled
from catalogues and brochures
each detail bragging status.

There's no circle of rocks,
no sign to give an outward form
to the phantoms, the whisper of stories.
I want a place to mourn the dead
fighting with spears against guns,
to mourn the corrosive
murdering hatred.
I want a space away from the houses,
simple but rich in memory
a place we all share

to conjure a beauty back to this place.
The killers wash off the blood
and return to the hugs of wives and children
living in wooden shacks.
They dream of homesteads
with wraparound balconies,
multiplying to a clustering
of swollen mansions
slowly growing down the generations.
I want to smash them
but I only have my words.
My fury shifts into sadness.

BORA RING

on Gubbi Gubbi Land

I'm walking on a rough track
through rows of plantation pines
then a field of pineapples
sown in rigid lines.
In a clearing
near a blossoming bottlebrush
the grass rises in a curve then falls.
Clouds drift
shadowed with the promise of rain.
An outline sharpens
a rim of rounded earth
revolves with my eyes
its presence catches my breath
a perfect circle.
The ordered fields blur and vanish
only the ring is real
its centre flickers with shadows.
Wind hums through the bottlebrush
a flapping of wings
like the skipping of my heart
birds twitter and chime.
I'm on the outside
my senses alert
but lulled in a rhythmic dream.

My breathing deepens
but nothing is solid
except the circle's simplicity
a reflection of the moon.
A place of listening.
The ring widens.
On the horizon the Glasshouse Mountains,
steeples and rounded pavilions
quiver in sharp focus.
A forest regenerates on the rolling plain
as the sky brightens and darkens.
They gather to share.
Story is ceremony.
Togetherness.
A rite of passage for the young.
The song deepens with every repetition
a myth I will never know.

BUNYA

on Wakka Wakka Land

As I sit with waving ferns
the crooked limbs of eucalypts
the bunya towers
straight as the column of a temple,
its trunk like weathered stone
but alive,
grey flesh of a reptile
rough with multi-coloured speckles
giant remnant of ancient time.
I crane my neck dizzy
the bunya touches the sky
way above the daily life of the forest.
I hear the humming of sap
as the tree rises through the canopy
shooting out slim fingers
opening like hands
forming wheel after wheel.
Spokes burst open with blooms,
clusters of blue-green prickles
like anemones in the sky.
They spread wide, then taper to a point.
The ferns, the crooked eucalypts
bow down before the bunya's towering dome.

MY GREAT-GRANDMOTHER

Conondale, Queensland 1900 on Gubbi Gubbi Country
based on a story my mother remembers hearing…

She must get to Maleny!
She's riding in a buggy
the driver whips the horse
she wears a smart bonnet.
She warily reaches under her silken blouse
her hand can trace a little foot
through her porous skin, she caresses
her swelling so gently, she delights in a kick.

One of her husband's men is driving.
Why isn't he here? So often away to rule the world,
back tomorrow, but my labour is now.
I must get to Maleny!

The buggy lurches on the pitted track
it's like a blow; she hunches over to protect her.
(It's a girl, I'm sure) Please! Take care!

The sky is closing over.
Light is falling in strands through a tangle of branches.
She looks back at cattle grazing on thick lush grasses
the undulating fences, the river curving through the valley,
their cottage in a garden of daffodils, a walnut pianola.
It all disappears, now there's only

thickening trunks, rough bark wrapped in vines,
fresh shrubs and blossoms in red and blue
shoot out from the rot of fallen branches.
Serrated leaves scratch her face
shaped like hearts with a border of crimson,
they sting as the track narrows and rises.
This land does not belong to me!

A tingle rises through my back
my belly is squeezing,
spasms roll in waves from top to bottom
the baby is squirming
this pain will kill her!

The sky disappears
hidden by boughs and creepers
dangling and strangling.
I'm choking.
My bonnet tips off
hanging on its red ribbon.
Nowhere I can go, I'm out of control.
I'm shaking and lurching like the buggy
I must get to Maleny!
The driver whips the horse,
the pain is now less.

How I want the crisp sheets of my bed
protected by velvet curtains
a mosquito net
my husband holding my hand,
everything in its place.

The baby gently kicking,
emerging with my breaths.

A frog croaks, then another, then a hundred.
Insects buzz and hiss like boiling,
I cannot see them, a sickness in their throats.
A crow shoots up from a grey cluster of ferns,
black circles hover in deepening shadows.
The branches convulse.
The pain is sucking me down
and as I float above myself
the last strand of light at the end of day
squeezes through the canopy.

I see eyes sparkling with a playful challenge–
thick beard like a leprechaun
full lips open to speak.
Maybe he's here to soothe me.
There's a red spot on his forehead
trickling with blood.

She'll be the perfect young lady,
her dresses bright in delicate fabric.
She'll play Beethoven and sing;
she'll ride in a mahogany carriage drawn by shining horses;
she'll learn algebra at the best school in Brisbane.
I won't let her walk in this forest.

The leprechaun dances, pulling a sapling up with its roots.
Blood gushes down his cheeks.
Overhanging leaves brush my face, down to my belly.

I beat them away,
wrapping my arms and body around my girl and screaming.
The driver follows her demented eyes. He picks up his gun.
"No! Please! No!"

He chuckles.
"It's a rock! It can't be a native. Your father got rid …."
"Stop! Please stop!
You're hurting my daughter.
It's no longer moving! My baby is no longer moving!"

Ahead is a rock, pocked with sockets,
a stubble of moss, a red mark like a ruby at the top.
She stares at it in a silent plea.
Just as the last light fails, the rock quivers,
the windless forest blackens.
She kicks! The baby kicks!
The spirit blessed my child!
Pain tears through her again.
She is the only thing that matters!
My father is a good man.

I must get to Maleny!

SEARCHING FOR BRIDGET

(in 1929 Bridget moved to a new property near Goomeri on Kamilaroi Land)

Deirdre and I
are here to search for Bridget Ahern
my great-grandmother,
to walk on her land
to find her story, my mother's story.
She was here for a year in 1942; she was ten,
sent here from Brisbane to keep her safe from war.
She's never been back.

"I remember this hill."
Rows of fence posts
stranded with taut barbed wire
rise and fall in waves of dull green grass
dying to brown, stranded with thistle.
Then a single broken tree at the top of the hill.
Like a naughty child, I climb through the gate,
huffing middle-aged; I'm not a trespasser,
this is her country, part of my story.
At the top of the hill
more tame grasses rolling forlorn,
a few lonely trees, crows fossicking.
Is this all that's left?
The bunya forests are an hour's drive away,
but here?

I'm getting to know you, Bridget.
I'm reading you from your country.
No secret places, no lively forest pockets.
I count the cattle, lounging and fattening.

This is what she saw,
riding on a thoroughbred;
all hers
she is satisfied.

I feel her jealousy to control her land–
it's just feed for the cattle.
All mystery has been erased,
nothing to make me gasp, nowhere to ramble.

Except – shadows of stockmen,
black faces in cast-off clothes
hammer in fence posts, clear a patch of scrub
in endless repetition, heads down,
resigned to her scrutiny. They dream a forest.
They keep the land productive and their mistress rich.
"It hasn't changed at all," my mother says.

HOMESTEAD

"Where was the homestead?"
"It burned down in the 50s."
"Oh. What was it like?"

"I can't remember."
Then teasing fragments, snapshot images:
Climbing hibiscus, blooming jacaranda,
a long cool veranda, wide expansive lawn
with a rocking horse, croquet rings.
A multi-coloured rose garden,
no flowers from the forest—
their growth would be too precocious,
strangling the delicate daffodils.
A native is clipping the hedges.

Shining steel curves in green,
bulbous headlights, a high silver grille.
All the details are forming a picture
now quickening with life.

George – my great-grandfather – bought a new car every year.
He's standing beside it in leather gloves, white shoes
prosperous belly in a striped shirt, twirling moustache, always tipsy.
Other cars arrive, boxier, larger,
growling engines outdo each other.
The guests step out; swagman's hats with gold watches,
swirling dresses with diamond bracelets, the sparrows scatter.

"Oh, Charles, you always make things up;
they were hmm… not like that at all."

Bridget always at the centre, a head taller than George.
My mother runs towards her,
her ribboned ponytails come up to her heart.

Bridget picks her up and twirls her,
she feels her strong arms; she can chop wood,
change a tyre. Nan can do anything!
A woman in command!

I sniff the lace, the corseted dress
a locket with the holy virgin,
her chin with a pouch like a frog.
I caress the powdered lines under her eyes.
I want the rest to go away so I can hear her stories
of love-smitten maidens and leprechauns.

We enter the dining room.
A yellow table with brown swirls,
glowing white plates adorned with roses
the smell of roasting beef.
Nan says her ironwood stove is the latest.
It's all so much bigger than our house in Brisbane.
We're served by a maid

nobody notices her because she's black
but she's not much older than me,
so I try to catch her eye; she looks away.

Braying voices, fists pound the table.
The men are becoming heated,
blood dribbling on chins, peeling laughter.
I catch the maid's eye–
this time she smiles at me.
I roll my eyes, but she runs back to the kitchen
as my Nan barks an order.
She never stops, my Nan, nor do the maids.
Plates disappear, new plates arrive. Nan is in command.
"The men talk, but women do things. I want this lunch to be perfect!"

The scene is spinning out of control.
Their sons are at war, but they're talking eugenics,
sloping skulls, features like gorillas—
the only thing they understand is a gun.
Who are their sons fighting? People just like them.

With a war on, prices are sky-high!
Did you see my new car? My prize bull?
That maid is ripe.
I talked to the minister, the Premier agrees.

At last I'm with my Nan again.
"I'll leave them to clear away,
but heaven knows they still don't know how to clean.
I need to watch their every move. Sometimes they just take off.
Good help is so short!"

They're on the veranda, and Deirdre's holding a book.
"What kind of wisdom will that offer her?
Does she not realise that poverty is always waiting to pounce?
I was one of fourteen; I had to fight for everything!

Such a beautiful girl, she snuggles against my chest.
Clever like her mother, who almost died in the forest.

Her mother, such a singer, such a pianist.
I gave her everything to make her shine.
She threw herself away on a rude little clerk
with only a handsome face to his name!
She said he was every maiden's dream
but he's a vulgar nightmare, always asking me for money.
Deirdre is my treasure. I want her to be strong.
I want her to be better, kinder than me!"

BLACK COCKATOO

She walks past the roses
(her mama loves roses)
and rests on the grass,
pulling the ribbons from her hair
so it falls free, touching her cheeks.
The grass is so soft
it'll stain her cotton dress.
Grandma won't like it

Grandma is perfect.
She never stops
the voices braying around her,
the cranking engines.
Here, at last, it is quiet.
She's alone.
She picks up her book.

She's free to wander the skies
on a magic carpet encrusted with jewels
to land in Paris, nothing like here;
gargoyles staring from a cathedral.
But they're friendly, they'd listen to her
like the men in berets sharing talk in cafes.

Much better than her mother and father arguing at home!
Her eyelids droop; she's high above it all
until she drops back into the garden with tears on her cheeks.

Then I see them.
The three maids
on the other side of the lawn,
concealed from the house by a hedge.

They're breathing together, holding hands,
their bodies spread in exhaustion
after their endless chopping, scrubbing, wiping.
They lounge in the soft grass – like me!
A whisper, then a giggle.
What are they laughing at?
Probably at grandma.
I want to laugh, too.

I raise my head.

They sense me and freeze.
They're not allowed to talk to me
even to look at me.
I get up to leave them in peace
but I hesitate

as the younger one shoots me a smile.
They want me to stay!
We're surrounded by flowers; the sun is setting.
We sit awkwardly in silence, not knowing what to say

then a happy gasp as they turn and stare
so utterly still.
I follow their eyes

to a black cockatoo
cracking a nut with his beak,
blazing red feathers in his tail.
He spreads his wings wide
as he takes off and hovers, watching us.

Time stops – we're sharing the thrill, breathing together.
Could I fly like that – with them?
The house would be tiny from so high above!
I leap up, opening my arms.
Their laughter hoots.
The younger shows me a flick of her tail,
flexing her arms like wings as she runs, as if to say
"This is a cockatoo."
I run after her.

"I'll race you!" she says.
"Where?"
"As far as you can go." She gives me a start.
I'm a hopeless sprinter at the convent.
Her long legs are flailing
the wind from them hits me.
I fall, my dress spattered with mud.
She turns to me, beaming.

She offers her hand to help me up
but I do it myself.
Aren't we supposed to be superior?
I've lost my book; I dropped it on the grass.
She picks it up, but, instead of giving it back,
she's looking at the pictures inside.

They gather around, cooing.
"Is this your country?" one asks, pointing at Notre Dame.
"No, it's far away in Paris. It's where I want to go."
"You're not from here. Did they take you away?"
"I'm from Brisbane. Grandma brought me here.
Where is your country?"

One points north, one points south, one points west.
I thought they were sisters. The younger one says,
"I'm from Cape York. My mother is there. I want to go back."
"My mother's in Brisbane. I want to go back, too."

A silence.
The cockatoo is on the lawn
preening layers of glowing black feathers.
We watch together
our faces now orange in the sunset.

"Get back to work!"
It's my grandma.
She's standing tall, black with purple lace,
like the cockatoo but frightening.
The maids shudder – her voice is like a blow.

The bird squawks and flies away
as they scatter back to the house.
"Deirdre. Come here."
I expect her to raise her hand.
She picks me up.

"I've told you, do not talk to native girls."
There's a fury in her eyes.
I nod.
"You'll understand one day."
(But my mother never did.)

Bridget sighs.
Her granddaughter and the maids
laughing together – at a black cockatoo!

Oh, the dirt on her glowing white dress!
Is this the future?
Everything she's built
is starting to unravel.
Here, everyone knows their place.
She knows her tasks; the cows must be milked,
the butter churned, dinner must be served.
If she stops, she glimpses a chaos
like the forest where her daughter almost died.
She feels a surge of fury. She'll put those girls on short rations.

She'll get her husband to shoot the cockatoo.
Deirdre looks up at her. How she loves her.
She wants to go to Paris!
I've never left Queensland.

A woman with a mind of her own
is a dangerous thing.
For a moment, she glimpses a freer world–
what a life she will have!

Then she grasps Deirdre's hand.
No, the only safe place is here.

I'll find a handsome young grazier for her.
They'll have a homestead like this.

CHERBOURG

We approach.
I feel a dread.
An hour's drive from Bridget's property
and yet my mother never heard the name.
It wasn't a word you said in front of children
a shadow that revealed too much,
defined by knowing glances, clicks of the tongue.
Then silence – the only solution to the native problem.
I'd never heard of it either
and yet I sensed it at the core of who we are,
a constriction in my throat.
I always avoided Australian history,
immersing myself in other imaginings.
It's taken me sixty years to make a start on this poem.

Cherbourg:
now just another town.
A cheerful woman shows us around
the settlement in all its details.
Immersed in the truth, she can smile.

At the centre, a room, a large desk.
Files with every detail of the inmates,
the latest books on the science of eugenics.
The Protector sat at this desk for forty years,
building an apparatus of total control
over every aspect of First Nations peoples' lives.

They were brought from all over Queensland,
the aim – to erase their memories and ways of living.

The girls are assembled in a photo.
They smile in grey uniforms, their hair cut short.
They were taken from their families on the fringes of towns.
The farmers had stolen their hunting grounds and land,
the memories of resistance and massacres were raw.
If the parents were seen as trouble, they were taken, too
and kept in a separate compound; they rarely saw their children.
No spaces between the beds in dormitories
no personal possessions, just their smocks.
Girls from all different nations thrown together.

They weren't allowed to speak their languages,
to speak back to a white man, even to look him in the eyes.
All reminders of their culture stripped away,
like a bonfire of books, a slashing of paintings.

Loud bells would wake them at dawn.
Total control over every moment!
A matron with a birch for the slouchers,
signs of uncleanliness, any hint of defiance.
They were taught their letters, chanting in huge classes;
no individual nurturing, no faith in them.
They were trained in needlework, mopping, and chopping,
nothing to spark imagination or dreams—
no music, no poetry, no history.

And yet, as they look into the camera
there's a complicity – they sense each other.

They've grown up together; they look out for each other.
They're sisters from different nations,
nursing a defiance of the endless scrutiny
telling their stories in whispers
in pauses between their exhausting tasks.
At thirteen, they're ready to be sent out to work.

What is evil?
To crush what's beautiful and deeply felt.
To disparage anything that's distinctive or different—
stories, languages, and dances—
with years of cold, methodical intimidation.
A kind of conversion therapy
to make them hate who they are
to break them, to hollow them out
to work without complaint for minimal wages,
teaching them to worship the greed that destroyed them.

My breathing quickens, my stomach churns.
I drop my pen. I pick it up. I read some more.
I imagine my ancestors entwined in
this search for status and control, the unending anxiety
that's in my DNA.

I'm sure Bridget was a regular visitor.
The girls were sent out as maids
the boys as labourers and stockmen.
She wanted ones she could train
with the energy to work from dawn to dusk.
The Protector lined them up so she could take her pick.
And so cheap! The meagre wages were paid to Cherbourg

to pay the camp's costs, the rest to a trust account,
a pittance for them. No leisure, no drinking
no time to find their voice and their fury.

"A cup of tea, Mrs. A…"
The Protector is jovial.
"Delighted, Mr. Bleakley. You're doing an important job."
They understand each other.
Nothing needs to be stated:
they click their tongues, shake their heads, and smile.
An efficient organiser is needed.
Mr. Bleakley is sweating in his suit,
careful and formal like a bank manager.
He puffs himself up; he's been the Protector for forty years.
Her husband is the Chairman of the Queensland Country Party.
The Premier and all the movers and shakers
are regular visitors to their homestead.
His job is safe from the bleeding hearts and troublemakers.
They bluster, full of righteous virtue
to cover their ceaseless anxiety
that their status and wealth can be ripped away.

STOCKMEN

She's mounted on a thoroughbred,
a posse of stockmen are on horseback behind her.
Some of them have worked for her for years.
They hardly speak. She spits out instructions
then a nod of their heads as they do her bidding.

There can be no intimacy.
Any question about their families
about the land they were born on and its stories,
would open up scars
touch on trauma so deep
it cannot be spoken of
except in a catharsis of fury and tears.

They're not allowed to look her in the eyes.
She's a good woman, a mother of five
a generous hostess, a pillar of her church
but she shuts down a part of her brain
with them. She becomes a psychopath.

She sees their pain in flickers; it hits her like an itch
but then she sees her tranquil homestead, her cattle grazing.
She shouts an order; the itch is gone.
She bursts with pride, how hard her family has worked
to build all of this; the land is now useful.

The stockmen know who she is,
about what her father did to steal their land
to clear it of anything holy,
about her powerful husband, a great advocate for Cherbourg.

They know the land better than she does.
They want to give her advice
about retaining stands of forest, some bunya trees
to add to its energy and productivity.

She cannot listen.
And yet there are moments
when she sees their care for the calves—
they know them all by name—
does she feel a flicker of respect, of compassion?

They're on the same land, but so far apart.
An uneasy silence between them.
Has anything changed?

PIANO ACCORDION

The last greasy plate has been cleared.
Grandchildren run boisterous.
The men light cigars, the women sip sweet wine.
Now is the time
after all her tasks are over
to tell them who they are
to share these precious songs.

She's now waiting for silence,
the accordion at her breast.
She squeezes the bellows;
her fingers with emerald rings on the keys.
The sound is warm, quickening to a dance—
high like a squeal, then a low braying.

Her rigid stance softens.
Can she reach the notes to conjure
a maiden's yearning
as she waits in perfumed heather?
The sunshine turns to shadow,
she knows he will never return.

The men wink, a woman giggles,
a child is running under the table.
She strides over to give him a wallop
then she searches on the squeeze box

singing among the wild roses.
The river flows clear, a mist on the fields;
she wants them to see
rainbows and mischievous elves.

Suddenly she slows, she misses the high notes,
the words start to jumble
and none of them join in.

These songs of feasting and famine!
The spirit of Ireland!
The joy in her father's eye as he played
her grandfather's favourite song!
She quickens her fingers, feet tap a rhythm.
She twists in a reel; she defies
the English boots tramping on her country—
cottages burnt, heroes hanging like dogs from trees,

the Irish landless and voiceless.
These songs are all they have.
How well her father could dance!

They remain seated, hiding their yawns.
What is it with all these bonny dead lasses,
brown eyes shining in the mist
the rainbow pouring from your lips?

Here the sun is bright, the cattle are fat.
We're all white and free!

As she squeezes the accordion more forcefully,
she finds in its dark shimmering notes
something that has been left behind.
Her voice quickens; she finds a gentleness.
We have our homesteads, our cars
the fancy dresses and hats from shops in Brisbane,
but what of the green shades where love begins?
Where is our spirit?

For a moment I like you, Bridget, you're in my DNA.
I searched for love in a city stricken with plague.
I perform my songs, defying the oppressors.
I would have loved to hear you sing.
They called you a battleaxe, but I admire your passion.
My mother said she didn't like the way they mocked you.

Except you missed the most important thing:
the spirit of this country.
It was standing right beside you;
a First Nations maid sweeping the floor,
watching for the flying hand of her mistress.

As you ordered the stockmen to cut down the bunya trees
to clear a new paddock, you did not see their tears.
You diminished yourself as you diminished them,
so your songs lost their meaning.

It's left to me to find you again – in poetry.

PART THREE

SACRED LAND

HIDDEN PASSAGEWAY

written on Gundungurra Land

1.

Faraway
a myopic blur of treetops
sliced in two
by a winding creek.
The valley is unreachable
from the rough ledge
on which I sit,
a death drop
down a sunbaked cliff
except
in the shadow of twisting banksia branches,
the jagged rock is torn
by a deepening slash.
The banksia stands guard,
a mess of crooked limbs
knobbly cobbs bristling with seeds.
I push its coarse branches aside
and see a gaping mouth,
a steeply descending path—
a hidden passageway
in an ancient ruin.
As the shade deepens
a blue beetle scuttles,
whiskers of green

sprout out of bumps.
It's cool
inside this monstrous rock
split by a million storms
burrowing their way
to the creek below.
The steps are slippery
my boots squelch yellow with mud.
A giant tree trunk
covered with turquoise moss
has toppled from above.
I look up
to a neck of rock
bridging the crack,
ribbons of vines dangle.
Down, down
step by step.
A doorway is ahead,
glowing with greenness.

2.

A waterfall glistens
bouncing over rough-hewn terraces.
The passage widens to an alcove.
At the bottom
ferns tangle with wildflowers
around a clear pool,
a garden is feeding
on soil washed from the ridges.
Leaves sharpen and quiver
in the glare of midday sun.

Four tall trees
are dwarfed by the cliffs:
coarse rock baked burnt orange,
pocked with sockets
slit with grinning cuts,
thin shrubs cling to it like stubble.
Everything is present
deep in this pocket.
A leaf tapers to a point
rounded pebbles are churned by the stream
purple buds are opening on crooked stems
boughs twist upwards.
A song hums
somewhere in my head,
a motif repeating
like textures on rock
fern fronds and flowing water.
Where does it come from?
I do not know.
It echoes from the distant past
into the future.

ANVIL ROCK

Monolith
towering over the forest canopy

its surface rolls in bulges like resting muscles
black grooves swirl deep into orange gristle,

streaked with sulphur, shrubs tremble on precarious ledges.
Light oscillates as the clouds drift,

bruised cauliflower heads stained with sweat
scattering feathers into the glaring blue.

On the roughness of the faraway cliff,
two smudges quiver like stick men waving.

At my feet, a flannel flower
white buds clustering on a stalk like jewellery.

SUNSET AT HARGREAVES

No longer blinding,
the sun dazzles
a ball cut in two
teetering
on the jagged rim
of undulating mountains.
Trees are sharpening
into silhouettes,
the cliffs gleam
streaked with looming shadow
as slowly, slowly
the sun is sinking
still shooting with flame.

High in the sky
the clouds are running yokes
of clotted cream
shifting in shape,
trailing a haze of sparks.
Their colour deepens
even as they are fading.

You're so still
as you stand
in amazement.
Your gaze shifts
then you're transfixed again,

the lines of your body
washed in orange.
Your wonderment grows in me.
Then I turn.
The full moon's white
becomes visible
against the deepening blue.

A FLASH OF WHITE

I'm alone in the forest
my breath twisting like a bramble,
thorns but no leaves
knotted in a tangle.
I'm picking at old scabs
as my eyes search the trees.

Then far away
amid precariously bending boughs,
a flash of white
a new breath
joins with a naked trunk
like marble shining
in a motley of shadows.
The sun dazzles
stepping from the clouds.
I glow
a thrill in my breath
as branches –
quivering lines of white
like spines of feathers –
rise above the canopy
then a whisper of comfort,
a caress in words like
'All will be well'.
The tree resonates
as brambles twist at my feet.
I want to speak like you.

GOVETTS LEAP AT NIGHTFALL

A silhouette emerges
a sleeping head,
the blackness of rock
resting on a thundercloud
and deep down below,
the texture of trees
patterned like porcelain,
a darkening fabric
over waves on the valley floor.
Droplets jostle there
weaving in a strange magnetism,
balls and slipstreams of mist
not solid, but present
moist, but not liquid
joined in cold energy.
Like a long sighing
the sound of water
falling unseen
down a jagged cliff.
Everything is a hint
of what it is
swaddled in greyness,
fertile, pulsing.

FISH PARK AT GARRAGUL (ELIZABETH BAY)

The words drain of meaning
rigid on the page.
I'm tired of stories.
Books slide from the shelf
and gather in mounds.
I feel desire
not for a person
but for a merging,
a flowing of shapes
to quicken my breath.
It cannot happen here;
I picture a garden.

Streetlights at equal paces
the buildings loom
in their ornate pomposity.
Bitumen of road
is washed with a layer of yellow,
rainbows of light
cold and flickering
in the windows.
Can I be fascinated?

A trembling rhythm:
buzz buzzing cicada

the hoot of a bird
the skipping flow of water
a stone bridge like a sigh.
All is suggestion.

The buildings fade.
A dark globe
is above me now.
Shadowy puffs float
like tarnished silver
lit faintly from within.
Bumps and furrows
glimmer like thinking.

Swirling clouds
glisten in bunches
a radiant sphere peeps out
and is swallowed again,
the wind hits my cheek.
The sky is aroused
gliding with a slow momentum.

My breathing deepens
the focus sharpens.

A circle of thorns
then another
break open from a stalk.
Slithers of metal
moist with a bluish sheen
are as pliable as petals.

Above the stalks,
a purple glow
flows into the distance.
The harbour ripples
flashing with red, smudges of grey,
boats are bobbing like toys.
Fingers like buildings
are pierced with pinpricks of light.
Jagged peninsulas are floating
in grey water spumed with colours.

A ball sits on the lawn,
the fleece of its surface
is shorn and pruned
into a rounded hedge.
Swarms of leaves like tiny fish
feed up and down the twigs
wriggling and shaking.
illuminated by—

The moon is full,
astonishing.
As it emerges
the clouds become faint,
a path vibrates on the water.

An intake of breath and laughter—
like someone I love beside me.
I've awakened.
I sense beneath surfaces.

Leaves are shining with mauve
petals fall
in flashes of pink.
A spray of reeds
bursts from the lawn
jostling in the lunar light
like it's seaweed
at the bottom of the harbour.
The wind has the thickness of water.

Whispers are leaping in song.
I can almost see them.
The Gadigal women are at home here
sitting in a circle
weaving stories
from moon, leaves, and sky.
I feel their presence
in everything.
This was a holy place.
It's still a holy place
deep inside the city.

AFTERWORD

I put distinctive voices and big stories at the heart of my third collection, *Sacred Remnants*. I continue the work in *Dining at the Edge* and *The Crumbling Mansion*, writing about the provoking complexity of mavericks I've met around Kings Cross. Knowing them has always been an antidote to the grinning conformity of life in Sydney. They are a little like the savants in Patrick White's *Riders to the Chariot*, unseen by most, but they enrich and unsettle the people they come into contact with. They are often despised, seen as misfits and outsiders. They are strong women like Elizabeth Burton, Candy, and Mae, trans and nonbinary like Ayesha, Jessie, and Charlotte, gaining strength and resonance from their mixture of masculine and feminine characteristics. They are under threat; some of them are dead. They are freewheeling individuals; they're not afraid of dangerous ideas. They have an uncanny presence on the page. I channel them with vivid imagery and rhythm; they come to life in me. I describe the sacred energy of performance spaces like the Rattler and Les Girls, of reciting Shakespeare and the Mardi Gras parade. I write about places I saw on a trip to England as well. I'm seeking something that rises above the overpriced blandness of Sydney. There are several long poems; the stories are surprising and complex, mixed with short lyric poems.

Sacred does not mean supernatural. It's what we feel when we meditate on the multilayered colour, texture, and lushness of an unspoiled landscape. We erased First Nations culture and stories, so full of powerful spirituality; then we denied this spirituality existed as we took over the country. As we destroyed, we diminished ourselves. My mother's family were the first invaders in Queensland in the 1860s; they played their part in this over generations. The sacred is left only in remnants, in people and places I write about.

So my second task is a reckoning with the brutal dispossession of First Nations people through the story of my family in Queensland. I describe the destructive process of stealing land, the massacres, and the erasure of First Nations stories and memory in places like Cherbourg. I tell the story through the eyes of two powerful women: my mother as a girl and my great-grandmother Bridget Ahern. Both are hurt by the prevention of any intimacy between black and white people. They are part of the abuse of First Nations maids and stockmen, working for meagre pay that was often stolen. So, Bridget, the racist settler, is diminished by the wealth she builds, full of anger and anxiety, losing connection with her Irish culture as her songs become laughable and irrelevant. Her pragmatism drains anything sacred from the land around her. Yet she too is a powerful presence like the women in Part One. She's a victim, like all of us, of blinkered greed. Yet mavericks still exist: the eccentric women and nonbinary people whose stories are the spine of this collection. The bora ring, the bunya pine, and the Glasshouse Mountains remain, a reminder that this is still Aboriginal land. So, the final part, Sacred Land, is a kind of reconciliation, describing unspoiled landscapes in the Blue Mountains, with an energy that echoes from the distant past into the future.

HUMBLE THANK YOUS

It takes a village of loving supporters to produce a book of poetry. Deepest thanks to Stephen Edwards, Peter Urquhart, Judith Beveridge, Deirdre Freyberg, Lou Steer, Brian Martin, Marguerite Montes, John O'Driscoll, Tim Wright, Mary Burgess, Charlotte (Andy) Biggs, Danny Gentile, Gregory Dickerson, Candy Royalle, James Velocita, Simon, Fran and Grace Whitehead, Martin Richardson, Jessie Fuller, Matt Jennings, Wilfred Roach, Angela Stretch, Tug Dumbly, Kerri Shying, Dimitra Harvey, the poets of the University of Sydney Graduate Poetry Seminar, Stephen and Brenda Matthews, and David Reiter, my wonderful editor and publisher.

NOTES

"to Elizabeth Burton": Elizabeth Burton was a stripper at venues on Darlinghurst Road for over forty years. She became a mentor for queer performers like Emma Maye and Aaron Manhattan. Her costumes were designed by Mark Matou, who also designed for the performers at Les Girls. I became friends with her at the Picolo Café and remembered I'd seen her strip show and smiled when I was 16. She died in 2020.

"to Kate": In memory of Kate Vidgen, a surrealist painter and dear friend who died in 2019. The painting described in the poem still hangs on my wall. We often talked about the beautiful, abusive people we'd loved.

"to Jessie in Fish Park": To my non-binary muse Jessie Fuller, still very much alive.

"to Mae": This poem is based on a friend and amazing Kings Cross character. I retell her stories here with a dash of imagination.

"to the Bourbon and Les Girls": Ayesha was a performer at Les Girls on Darlinghurst Road and still rides her motorised wheelchair around the area with her two little dogs. She especially loves Shirley Bassey. She has appeared in the work of many other Kings Cross writers.

"Rattler": Thanks to Nicola Bailey and George Malouf, Candy Royalle's literary heirs, for allowing me to use short quotes and paraphrases from her book *A Trillion Tiny Awakenings* (UWP 2018). She introduced her gigs with "this is a Sacred Space"; it's written on the back of the book, and I've echoed phrases from "Not Another Love Poem" (p. 63) and "Our Hearts" (p. 117), "whispering poetry onto flesh" from "Citadel of Sighs" (p. 51). Thanks so much, Candy, for your kindness to me; I miss you so much.

"Stone at Five Fingers Strand": There's a mural on the walls of Derry for the people shot by British soldiers in the Bloody Sunday Massacre in 1971. Thanks to Matt Jennings for taking me to nearby Donegal in the Irish Republic to see Cape Malin, the northernmost tip of Ireland.

"White Horse": The Ridgeway was also the inspiration for Kate Bush's song "Running Down the Hill." The White Horse was first drawn in soft chalky soil in Bronze Age times, about 400 BC, near the ruined castle. Local artists (such as Martin Richardson) have regularly redrawn the lines ever since. Thanks to James Velocita for taking me there.

"Martin's Painting": An earlier version of this poem appeared in my book *Dining at the Edge*. I included it to give context on Martin. I met Martin and Jim in Kings Cross in the 1990s. They'd become friends with my dear friend and inspiration Mary Burgess. Her house and some of the people helped inspire *The Crumbling Mansion*. To all the beautiful people who died in the AIDS plague.

"Bewitched in the Park": An earlier version of this poem appeared in *Dining at the Edge*. I've been performing it along with other poems from this book with "The Fierce Violets" at the Sydney Fringe and other places, so I think it belongs in this book. Thanks to Charlotte (Andy) Biggs.

"Playing with Shakespeare": I lived in London for nine months in Kelfield Gardens, North Kensington, in 1986 when I was 21/22. I returned to the street on my recent visit for a few weeks in 2023. Quotes from Shakespeare are from *Richard II, Hamlet, Henry VI, Part 3*, and *Richard III*. Thanks to Simon, Fran, and Grace Whitehead for hosting me in London.

Evonne: Margaret Court was always kind to Evonne Goolagong and mentored her. She's an evangelical Christian and made a fool of herself attacking gay marriage during the plebiscite.

"My Great-Great-Grandfather": Joseph Macarthy (1838-1916) was an original settler of the Maleny area, Gubbi Gubbi country. My Ahern relatives in Brisbane say they "don't know" whether he was involved in Aboriginal massacres. Streets in Maleny are named after him. He arrived in the area in the 1860s. I found the black-and-white photo I describe in the poem in the State Library in Brisbane. I went for a tour around Queensland looking for signs of my family. I travelled with my mother, Deirdre Freyberg (1932-), and I enjoyed her many recollections, sometimes vague, but often enough to hang a poem on. I also did research in the State Libraries of Queensland and New South Wales.

"Mansions at Weyba Lake": I discovered this story in Eve Fesl's book *Conned* (UQP 1993) and other books in the Queensland State Library. There's a street of mansions near Noosa on Weyba Lake where the massacre took place. There's no memorial to mark the spot, even though scores were murdered there in the 1860s. I wanted to find the spot, but you can't walk through to the lake because the mansions take up all the land. An eyewitness account from a document in the State Library repeated in my head. There's a road called 'Murdering Creek Road' nearby. Loving condolences to the Gubbi Gubbi people on whose land it lies, and my deep apologies– because Joseph Macarthy was possibly involved, or at least knew about it and approved.

"Bora Ring": This Bora Ring is located at the edge of the Beewah State Forest in a pineapple farm near Landsborough. Humble thanks to the Gubbi Gubbi people for preserving it. The poem is my impressions as I sat by the ring. I consulted the Gubbi Gubbi people about this poem.

"Bunya": I visited the Bunya National Park on Wakka Wakka Country near Kingaroy and saw these glorious trees, sacred to the Aboriginal people of Queensland.

"My Great-Grandmother": This is based on a story told to me by my mother. Bridget Ahern, my great-grandmother (1878-1963), became "terrified" when riding through the forest from Conondale to get to the hospital in Maleny when she was in labour. She never felt comfortable in the forest again. The poem is from my imagination.

"Searching for Bridget": The Ahern family moved from Conondale to Tansey near Goomeri in 1929. Their homestead was called Lakeview; it was one of the largest properties in the area. My mother and I drove around the land trying to imagine Bridget. The poem about the homestead is based on a single photograph and my mother's recollection. She remembers the athletic skills of the Aboriginal maids on the property. "Black Cockatoo" is largely from my imagination, starting from a few remembered details.

"Cherbourg": Based on my visit to Cherbourg, many thanks to the guides, and also *Dumping Ground: A History of Cherbourg* by Thom Blake (UQP 2001). George Ahern, my great-grandfather, was an office bearer in the Queensland Country Party, who set up and supported the settlement. The stockmen and maids on their property came from Cherbourg. The constituency around Kingaroy, Joh Bjelke Petersen's old seat, voted 80% no in the Voice Referendum. They still don't want to hear Aboriginal voices there.

"Piano Accordion": Based on the recollections of my Ahern relatives in Brisbane about how they hated Bridget's piano accordion recitals of Irish songs. They were forced to listen to them as children. The songs obviously didn't speak to them. It made me see Bridget's vulnerability and that she, like the other women in the collection, was a maverick at heart.

"Hidden Passageway": These poems are a reconciliation with the sacredness of land, even after all the injustices we have inflicted on the First Nations people. They are based on my walks around the Blue Mountains. "Hidden Passageway" and "A Flash of White" are based on the area around Mermaid Rock near Blackheath. Hargreaves Lookout is just beyond Shipley near Blackheath. Many thanks to Peter Urquhart for his friendship and hospitality—his sense of a spiritual presence in land is a major inspiration for this collection. Thanks to the Gundunjurra people.

"Fish Park at Garrugul": This is a place where I often go walking and meditating; it's not far from where I live. It's just below Elizabeth Bay House. It's made up of many textured imported plants, a fishpond, and a bridge right by the harbour. It certainly has a magic about it, a sacred remnant, and a refuge in the middle of multi-million-dollar apartments. Rose, a First Nations friend in the Cross, told me it was a place for secret women's business at the time of settlement. At times, I feel a presence there.

ABOUT CHARLES FREYBERG

Charles Freyberg is a Kings Cross poet and performer. In the 1990s, he worked as an actor and director, especially with the surreal clown Victor Sheehan, his first poetic mentor. His own writing started with drag shows and performance art staged at Club Bent at the Performance Space in the late nineties and with several plays. He studied poetry at postgraduate level at the University of Sydney, supervised by Judith Beveridge. His poems have been published in *Meanjin, Plumwood Mountain, Urban Village, From Sydney to Bistrata*—an anthology of Sydney poetry translated into Romanian, the Sappho Queer anthology, and other local papers and websites. His books *Dining at the Edge* and *The Crumbling Mansion* were published by Ginninderra Press and are still available. His work has been widely performed, including a dance opera about Chelsea Manning in Peter Urquhart's *The Experiment* at the Sydney Conservatorium, *Vanessa and Friends*, a theatrical night of his poetry at El Rocco Kings Cross, *Museum of Fleas* at the Sydney Fringe, *Taken for a Ride* at the Surry Hills Festival, the Nimbin Poetry World Cup, and *The Fierce Violets*, a group of poets and musicians performing numerous gigs around Sydney and twice at the Sydney Fringe, where they were nominated for a Fringe Award. He performed *The Crumbling Mansion Show* as a one-person show in Sydney and Newcastle, channelling all the characters, all their genders. He received an award for his services to LGBTIQ+ poetry at the National Art School during Mardi Gras 2020. His work has been translated into Spanish by Maria del Castillo de Sucerquia and has appeared in *Heidra Journal* (Mexico), *Boheme Caribe* (Colombia), and *Ajkoki* (Costa Rica). *Sacred Remnants* is his third book.

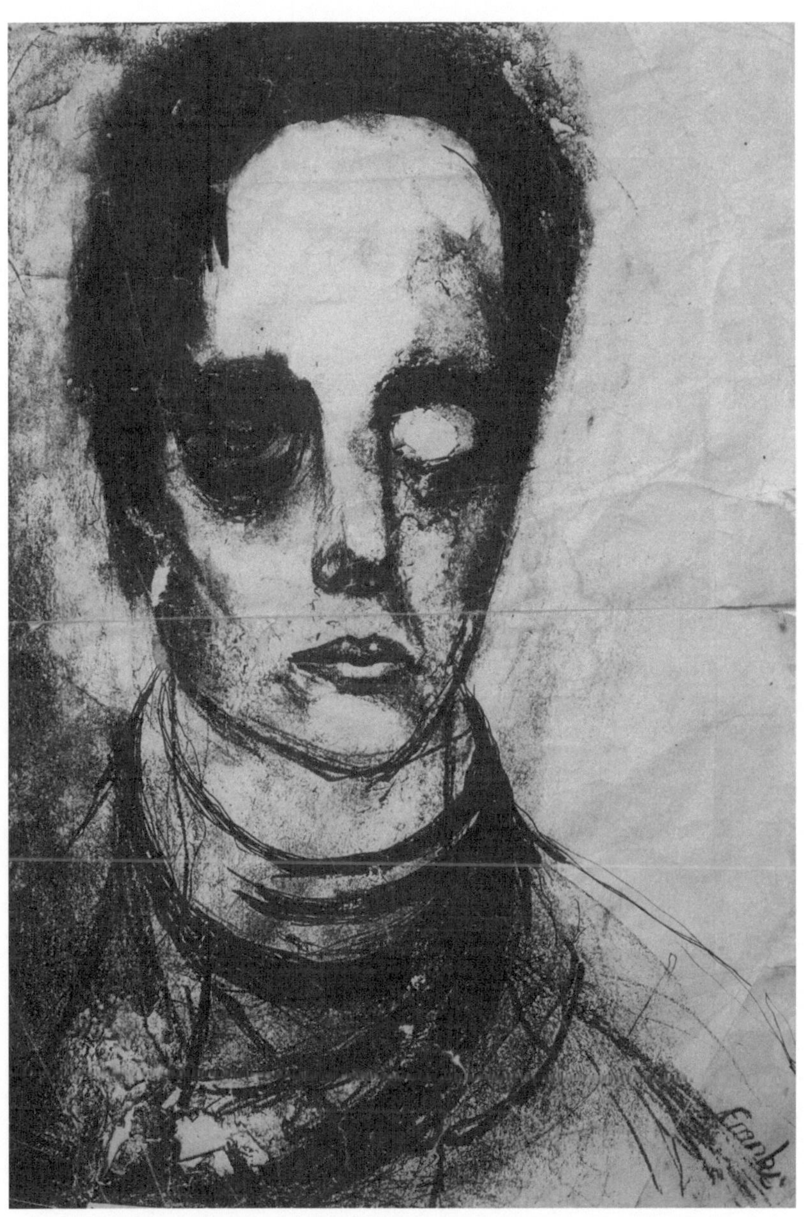

Author drawing by Margaret Franki (1986), ink on paper